Accla

Responding to ~~....~~ *~~....vent,~~*
Christmas and ~~....~~

These brief, humane and inclusive homilies, peppered with dry humour, unfold the paradox of a Christ-like God who stoops to heal his wounded creatures and wash their feet. *Church Times*

Dust that Dreams of Glory: Reflections on Lent and Holy Week
Marked by his characteristic economy of language, and an enviable ability to convey theological insight and pastoral wisdom with humanity, clarity and unshowy learning, and an utter lack of preacherly condescension. This is not theology incorporated into preaching, but theology that is formed in the act of preaching, and every word counts.
Church Times

Alleluia is Our Song: Reflections on Easter and Pentecost
As always and enviably, Mayne speaks with a hard-won simplicity of what he has found to be the central truths of the faith. *Church Times*

Giving Attention

Becoming What We Truly Are

Michael Mayne

Edited, with an Introduction, by
Joel W. Huffstetler

CANTERBURY
PRESS
Norwich

© The estate of Michael Mayne, 2018
Introduction © Joel Huffstetler, 2018

First published in 2018 by the Canterbury Press Norwich
Editorial office
3rd Floor, Invicta House
108–114 Golden Lane
London EC1Y 0TG, UK
www.canterburypress.co.uk

Canterbury Press is an imprint of Hymns Ancient &
Modern Ltd
(a registered charity)
Hymns Ancient & Modern® is a registered trademark of
Hymns Ancient & Modern Ltd
13A Hellesdon Park Road, Norwich,
Norfolk NR6 5DR, UK

British Library Cataloguing in Publication data

A catalogue record for this book is available from the
British Library

978 1 78622 100 1

Printed in the United Kingdom by CPI Group (UK) Ltd

Contents

To John and Ann Woody

Acknowledgements

A warm note of thanks to Alison Mayne for her gracious support of my work on her husband's unpublished papers, and for our friendship.

Martyn Percy and Christopher Collingwood were most helpful in the early stages of this project.

Thanks to Christine Smith and the team at Canterbury Press for sharing my passion for bringing more of Michael Mayne's unpublished work into print.

The people of St Luke's Episcopal Church in Cleveland, Tennessee, have been wonderfully supportive of sabbaticals in 2009 and 2016, during which much of my research on Michael Mayne's unpublished papers has taken place.

Debbie Huffstetler has partnered with me at every stage of this project. Thank you, my love.

The royalties from this book are donated to Emmaus UK in honour of Alison Mayne and in memory of Michael Mayne.

Joel W. Huffstetler
4 July 2018

Foreword

Terry Waite

It is most appropriate that royalties from this book will be given to Emmaus, the charity for the homeless founded by a French priest the Abbé Pierre. The following poem sums up in a few words the man himself:

I see him now,
Striding forth
Along Parisian streets.
Unmistakably a cleric.
Beret,
White beard,
Cassock,
Eyes that pierced indifference
And warmed
With compassion.

No altar chained this man,
No Church controlled his life.
He was poor with the poor,
Sad with the sad,
Hopeful with the despairing.
He walked the Parisian streets
As Christ walked to Emmaus.

Michael Mayne in this eloquent series of four short reflections sums up exactly what lay at the heart of the Abbé's spirituality, which is to give attention to ourselves, to God and to other people.

In founding Emmaus, following World War Two, the Abbé gave practical expression to his beliefs. Central to the philosophy of Emmaus lies the understanding that all men and women, regardless of their culture, creed or ethnic identity, have their dignity as children of God. In his wisdom, the Abbé did not found a religious organization. It was never his intention to preach to the homeless. Rather he chose to walk alongside them and in so doing to enable them to experience something of the care and compassion that lay at the very centre of his faith.

In these four essays Michael Mayne, himself a priest, outlines a pathway that may be taken by all who seek to deepen and enhance their own lives. This is an ideal book to take away on a short retreat. The journey he suggests we might take is not easy. It can, however, be profoundly rewarding.

I can do no better than to quote the author's final words:

God calls me, gently, persistently, every day of my life, to give attention to what I am so that I may give attention to what others are too, and so, little by little, become what I truly am until the day when 'I wake up after his likeness and am satisfied with it'.

Terry Waite CBE
President, Emmaus UK

The poem 'Abbé Pierre' is taken from the book *Out of the Silence*, by Terry Waite.

Introduction

A recurring theme in the preaching and writings of Michael Mayne is the importance of the present moment. Many of us are prone to spending overly much time regretting the past, or in being anxious about the future, all the while Christ is present with us in the moment that is now. Each moment is a precious gift, a grace, and offers us the opportunity to experience God's loving embrace. As a God-given gift, each present moment is worthy of our full attention. In *Giving Attention: Becoming What We Truly Are*, Mayne invites us to be 'present to the presence of God, and only in this present moment is God present'. He notes that 'we are forever pushing through the present moment so that we hardly ever live in it'. The wiser choice is to give each moment our full attention in order to become our best selves, the person we 'truly are'. Mayne reminds us that Jesus didn't speak much about people 'seeing God', but 'over and over again he pictured God at the heart of ordinary experience'.

In this set of addresses, many of the key themes of Michael Mayne's pastoral theology are touched on with arresting brevity and clarity. Readers will come away with a renewed appreciation that the extraordinary may be found in the seemingly ordinary.

1

A Golden Thread of Silence

Let me begin by explaining what I want to do and why I have chosen to call these addresses 'Giving Attention'.

I want to put before you a profoundly simple – that is to say, a simple but profound – truth. And it is this: that at root, the Christian life is about giving attention in order to become what we truly are. Prayer, spirituality, is about giving proper attention to God. Love is about giving proper attention to people, by which I mean attentiveness to what is before our eyes in the sacrament of each present moment.

I should define a religious person – one who is spiritually aware – as one who is prepared to give attention to the world, to its people and to its creator, in the process of learning to love them. Alan Ecclestone has pointed out in his book, *The*

Scaffolding of the Spirit: Reflections on the Gospel of John, that the root of the word 'religion' (the -lig-part) actually comes from a Greek word, *alego*, meaning 'to pay attention', 'to give care'; its opposite being the Latin *neglegere*, 'to neglect'. And what *we* are called to do is to pay attention to the mystery. 'People should think of us as Christ's servants' writes St Paul to the Corinthians, 'stewards entrusted with the mysteries of God'. And at the very end of *King Lear*, the old king says to the dead Cordelia that haunting phrase:

> (We'll) take upon us the mystery of things,
> As if we were God's spies.

How do we take upon us the mystery of things? By attentiveness. By opening ourselves in stillness to the mystery that each of us is. By opening our eyes to the wonder and mystery of the world. By giving attention to the mystery of God incarnate in the crucified and risen Christ.

I want to explore these mysteries with you in four ways: first, what it means to give attention to the God in whom we live and move and have our being at every moment, and then, second, what it means to give attention to the dark, to sin and pain and suffering and the God who suffers in Christ. Third, I want to talk about what it means to give attention to other people. And finally, what it ought to mean for each of us to give attention to oneself. You could call these four variations on the theme of giving attention: being, redeeming, loving and being loved.

So let me describe to you what things look like to me. Some of what I say may ring true for you as well, for while we are wonderfully different we are so alike. We may be Christians, but we are all sometimes bewildered and confused by the unpredictability and unfairness of life. We all sometimes get sick; we are not immune from pain and grief. We don't pretend to know all the answers. But what unites all of us most profoundly is the amazed discovery that, in the words of Paul Tillich, 'Here and there in the world and now and then in ourselves is a New Creation, usually hidden, but sometimes manifest, and certainly manifest in Jesus who is called the Christ.' What unites us is the belief that in the end, when we no longer see through a glass darkly, but, with astonishment and wonder, face to face, we shall discover that the meaning of it all will in fact be shown to lie in the mysterious truths God has disclosed in the life and death and resurrection of our Lord Jesus Christ.

I guess many of us find that life often takes us by the neck and sets us twitching. I know that as a parish priest (I hope I have learned better now) I used to spend quite a bit of time, in the psalmist's words, going around 'grinning like a dog' and (not in the psalmist's words) wagging my tail for approval. But we priests are actually not in the ministry to be frenetic organizers of this and that, nor to meet what may be false expectations of us, but first and foremost to be those who know how to be still, those who can be recognized as people who have, deep down inside them, a sort of contented stillness. Monica Furlong writes in her book, *Travelling In*, 'Priests are justified only by their powers of being and of seeing' – and I would extend that to include all who are seeking to be of service to others and help illuminate their lives.

Yet most of us find it very hard to come to terms with silence and to practise the presence of God. Being still and doing nothing makes us feel guilty.

I have in my study a quotation from Meister Eckhart, the fourteenth-century German mystic, which reads, 'Nothing in all creation is so like God as stillness.' And in the seventeenth century, Bishop Jeremy Taylor wrote, 'There should be in the soul halls of space, avenues of leisure and high porticos of silence, where God walks.'

Those familiar words from the King James version, 'Be still and know that I am God', are put rather more strongly in the Latin version, the Vulgate: '*Empty yourself* and know that I am God.' Human beings were not made for constant activity, a perpetual busyness, but the trouble is we don't know how to stop. We don't know how to listen to others or to God, because we are thinking about what we have to do next. We are forever pushing through the present moment so that we hardly ever live in it. Prayer, you might say, is a kind of hanging about until we catch up with ourselves. I remember Bishop John Taylor telling of how, when he was a missionary in Uganda, an African child walked into his office one day. He gave the child a brief greeting, but nothing more was said. The child sat there for a long time at John Taylor's feet while he carried on working. After about half an hour the boy got up and walked to the door, simply saying as he went, 'I have seen you.'

That's what being with God is like in stillness. It is being present to the presence of God, and only in this present moment is God present. For God only knows the present tense.

Surely we know deep in our heart that this is true, that it is 'in him that we live and move and have our being', that his Spirit is within us and among us. We know that our lives are to be a journey, a pilgrimage, as we slowly come to know for ourselves the great truths of the loving, forgiving, accepting God. Our whole life is to be, in Augustine's words, a 'becoming what you are', the liberated, redeemed, loved and valued child of God.

This act of re-creation has to happen every day. 'Come to me,' says Jesus, 'all you that labour and are heavy laden, and I will refresh you.' And in Latin 'refresh' is *re-facio*. I will *remake* you, I will make you anew. For a continuous creation and re-creation has to take place. And it takes time. It takes a lifetime, perhaps more than a lifetime. And it also takes the discipline of stillness, silence, being content to do less and to listen more. And there are no shortcuts.

What I am speaking of is not a private soul-making, an indulgence which the clergy and the professionally religious are lucky enough to have time for and others not. I am talking about a fundamentally different approach to life and to people, a different way of seeing, in which you take time to cultivate the interior qualities of silence, of looking and listening, for you know they are the only effective way in which you can discover God in the midst of your life.

There runs through the Gospel accounts of the ministry of Jesus a golden thread of silence. Jesus is the one who listens to the Father before he listens to people. His relationship with the Father is the beginning and the end of his ministry. His prayer, his time alone, his deliberate getting away from the crowds and even from the disciples, these – and the relationship of which they speak – lie at his very heart and are the secret of why people are then drawn to him. And when you think about his ministry, you wonder how it was that Jesus seemed to live without anxiety, even though he must have known from the start how it would end. How could he ride into Jerusalem on that first Palm Sunday with such calm assurance or tell his disciples on the very night of his arrest to 'set their troubled hearts at rest'?

It wasn't that he was incapable of a sense of desolation. His prayers at Gethsemane and his words from the cross show that he was as vulnerable as we are. No, it has something to do with his inner space, this practice of the presence of God. I find some words of Kierkegaard helpful here. He said that Jesus was able to live entirely without anxiety because 'He had eternity with him in the day that is called today: hence the next day had no power over him, for it had no existence for him.' That's one of the phrases I try (very unsuccessfully) to make part of me: 'He had eternity with him in the day that is called today.' That is to say, the future with all of its anxious questions loses its power and falls into perspective once you see this present moment in the light of eternity – once you know with absolute trust that you are held at this moment by the God who created all that is and who loves you and the person you are with and every other living being with an unchangeable love. And what is true of this moment will therefore be true of every subsequent moment of your life.

In a television programme on theories of creation and where the big bang theory places God, Rowan Williams said this:

> Aquinas wrote that it doesn't actually make any difference whether the universe has always existed or not. The point about the doctrine of creation is not that at a particular moment God said: 'All right: let's start it'; but that *at any moment imaginable* what *is* depends on God.

Unless God's creative power is at work in this instant,

everything collapses into non-being.

In his *Four Quartets*, T. S. Eliot meditates on the nature of time: time past, time future, time present. Eliot knows that no moment of time is isolated, that we carry all our past into what we are doing now, and that what we are doing now will affect in some small way our future, but what he is most concerned with is the intersection of eternity with time.

All this of course assumes two great truths: one concerning the nature of God, the other concerning me. What kind of God is it to whom we seek to open ourselves?

In one sense, he is an unknowable, incomprehensible God. The Jewish writer Isaac Bashevis Singer hit upon this charming metaphor for our place in God's universe:

> It is as if you were to ask a book-worm crawling inside a copy of *War and Peace* whether it is a good novel or a bad one. He is sitting on one little letter trying to get some nourishment. How can he be a critic of Tolstoy?

Yet we dare to pray to God because we believe this

hidden, reticent God once spoke in the only terms we can understand: in human terms, God with us, the Word made flesh incarnate in our midst. And our minds must somehow hold in tension the ultimate mystery of the transcendent God who is revealed as the Christlike God, the God whose life is within each one of us: the '*Abba*' of Jesus, the gracious intimate God who loves us for our own unique selves more than we can possibly know.

What sort of God? This sort of God: a God who calls us into wholeness through the daily rhythm of encounter and response that we call prayer.

My second assumption has to do with human nature. What kind of being are we? We are creatures in whom there is a kind of restless hunger: a sense of incompleteness, a search for wholeness beyond ourselves that goes beyond the search for a human partner. We are able to respond at the deepest levels we know to beauty in its many forms and to goodness and truth. In the words of Bishop Richard Holloway:

> I am dust and ashes, frail and wayward . . . quintessence of dust, and unto dust I shall return. But there is something else in me: an awareness

that, truly, I am not what I am; and what I am not is what I truly am. Dust I may be, but troubled dust, dust that dreams, dust that has strange premonitions of transfiguration, of glory in store, an inheritance that one day will be my own . . .

What sort of creature am I? One who will not be satisfied with anything less than the full vision of God.

The spiritual writer who has helped me most, and who seems to bring together many of my thoughts about giving attention to the hidden God who is capable of being found in every incident at the heart of his own sacramental world, is the eighteenth-century French priest, Jean Pierre de Caussade. The phrase by which he has become known is 'the sacrament of the present moment'.

De Caussade bases everything on the New Testament truth that God's nature is unchangeable, unconditional love, and that he cannot stop loving us any more than the sun can stop radiating heat. It follows, says de Caussade, that God's love comes to us through every single moment, that he is with us at this instant, whatever we may be doing or feeling or undergoing in this unpredictable world. His love doesn't come to us through what happened yesterday or what may happen tomorrow, but through this precise moment. Therefore, it is to this moment that we should give our whole attention, for, writes de Caussade, 'Every moment of our lives can be a sort of communion with the divine love.'

But if we are to know this, if we are to realize that at each moment we are held by a Love beyond our imagining, then we need to train ourselves to grasp this 'sacrament of the present moment'. And in two particular ways. We must root our formal times of prayer in the deep conviction that we walk through this world as those who are loved, until that truth permeates our whole lives. And we must learn to give attention, to concentrate, to focus down, to approach each moment as it comes – *this* person to be seen, *that* difficult letter to be written, *this* humdrum chore to be done, *these* addresses to be tackled. Which is difficult, but possible. 'We must cut off more distant views' writes de Caussade:

> We must confine ourselves to the duty of the present moment without thinking of what preceded it or what will follow it, for the duties of each moment are shadows beneath which the divine action lies concealed.

What I have been trying to say has to do with waiting

on God: with stillness, with listening – I suppose, in the end, with trust. Trust that God *is* and that, however unpredictable the world and whatever life may do to me, I am his loved and valued child. Bishop Michael Ramsey once spoke of how we can always see people:

> in the perspective of God, of heaven, of eternity. . . Anywhere, everywhere . . . God is to be found. In our daily encounters with people God is there . . . and we can be on the Godward side of every human situation. Yet we shall have the awareness of God and the power to be on the Godward side of every situation only if we carry with us into the day's ups and downs an interior castle of recollection drawn from our times of silence and eucharist and scripture. There is no by-passing the psalmist's wisdom, 'be still and know that I am God', and there is no by-passing the example of Jesus, whom Simon Peter found praying in a desert place a great while before day.

I guess that in the end, the giving of attention – to this moment, to who we are, to whatever we are doing and to whomever we are with – that giving of attention is not a bad definition of love. And therefore, it is also the surest, swiftest way to God who is both our journey and our journey's end.

2

Redemption

I wrote earlier about our need to discover in stillness the God in whose likeness we are made, and whose Spirit is within each one of us, of the need to learn 'to have eternity with us in the day that is called today' and in the sacrament of each God-given moment. But there is another side to the coin: human pain and suffering, and human wickedness.

I can only account for the hunger of the Spirit I find within myself if it is true that life is the gift of a loving creator, that I am created by Love for love, that I am to become what I truly am. Yet while part of my experience bears out that truth, the other part denies it utterly. The darkness is too close, the evil too sickeningly real: the Holocaust and the cancer cell; the terrorist bomb and the gloom of depression; the faces of the children in war-torn countries. And, for us all, the experience of sickness or pain or bereavement can make even our most transfigured moments seem no more than a self-deluding, selfish indulgence, powerless to affect the depth of anguish we may feel in the face of darkness. Then we resort to language that Flaubert likened to 'a cracked kettle on which we beat out tunes for bears to dance to, when all the time we are longing to move the stars to pity'. Which is why I look now to the God disclosed in Christ.

A Jesuit retreat conductor once began an address by pointing at the crucifix behind him and saying, 'What a way to run a universe!' We have to try to reconcile in our minds two apparently irreconcilable truths: the belief that God is in love with us, and our experience of suffering, pain and – sometimes – dereliction. I find it compelling that in their accounts of the crucifixion, Matthew and Mark only give us the one word of Jesus from the cross, the cry of desolation: 'My God, my God, why have you forsaken me?' For is it not precisely at this point that the nature of the God incarnate in this man Jesus is most sharply seen? Here is mystery indeed. Here in this dark hour is the divine pity revealed, God at one with all who for whatever reason feel they are forsaken.

I find this anguished cry of Jesus of such great

comfort because in it I hear the cry of all in our time who experience total darkness and alienation. Here the Passion of Jesus links with the passion of all men and women. The stories, the diaries and letters and poems of our time record many journeys that end in violent death: many hopes turned to dust and ashes. Surely the most potent figure of our time is the Jewish refugee whose journey ended not in the Promised Land but in the gas chamber along with millions of his or her fellow human beings. There are a few places the whole world knows – Golgotha; Belsen and Ravensbrück and Auschwitz; the old prison camps of Siberia; the Cambodia of Pol Pot; the Uganda of Idi Amin – and a thousand places where men and women, made like us in God's image and each of infinite and unique worth, are abused, tortured so that they may betray their friends, imprisoned for conscience's sake and killed.

Yes, the Passion goes on. And here is the strangest paradox, and to our minds the deepest mystery, that the crucified Jesus, who at this point knew to the full the ultimate isolation of the human spirit apparently cut off from God, is at the same time the only accurate picture of God the world has ever seen. If we believe that God is reconciling the world to himself by revealing his 'human face' in Jesus, then we must be willing to have our understanding of God profoundly changed. Here is a God who shares the dirt and the pain, the weakness and the loneliness, and the death that we experience ourselves.

I remember some words of Dame Cicely Saunders, one of the founders of the hospice movement, saying once in my church in Cambridge out of the depth of her long experience with the suffering and the dying:

> Surely all the hard things that have happened to anyone in his creation have happened to God himself. As any mother, seeing her child suffer, is suffering herself, so the Father of everyone has received all the sorrow and pain himself . . . and the presence of Jesus in history was the presence of God as he has always been and will always be.

I recall spending a week at Baylor University in Waco, Texas. It's the custom of the students there to use the pavements as a kind of university message service. They chalk on the sidewalk 'Happy birthday, John', or 'Tennis match, Monday at 6'. Crossing the road one day on my way to give an address, I was faced with these astonishing words chalked in large letters on the kerb: 'Jesus wept. Is your God man enough to cry?'

Like any priest or minister, I have celebrated both the joys and the sorrows of human life. In terms of the latter, I have sat with the dying, tried to console the bereaved, spent hour upon hour encouraging the unloved and listening to the wounded and the lonely. I have also known the dereliction of a long, debilitating illness, when it was almost impossible to pray at all. And all I know is that, for me, the only words that have helped have had to do with Christ crucified (or rather, the Easter Christ who still bears in his hands the marks of the nails and the wound in his side). The only words that I sense have helped others have had to do with the concept of the suffering God, whose love for each of us cannot be altered or diminished, and of whom I can say with the psalmist:

If I reach up to heaven thou art there: if I go down to hell thou art there also.

Let me then tell you as simply and honestly as I can both what the cross says to me about *me* and what the cross says to me about God. When I look into my heart, I know that I am hopelessly self-absorbed – egocentric. If I want to understand my own self-centredness, I only have to sit here and speak to you. For while part of me longs to speak of God in a way that will make the reality of his love more real for all of us, yet – if I am honest – I know that a small part of me all the while looks on and assesses how I am doing – beta plus, beta minus, gamma? – and is concerned – God forgive me – not so much with his value but my own.

You know this as well as I do. We refuse to be what we have it in us to be, sometimes deliberately, sometimes because we can't seem to help it. We have to say with St Paul, 'The good that I would I do not, and the evil that I would not that I do.' In a sentence, I stop short of that fullness of life I both desire and fear. Part of me longs to respond to God with my whole being, but part of me still dreads the thought of the whole of me coming together and saying 'yes' to God. 'Yes!', with nothing of myself left out, no holding back, no possibility of retreat.

And it is this holding back, this falling short, this fear, this concern with myself, this refusal to trust, that the New Testament calls *sin*. Sin is a kind of self-hatred: my ego fighting my true self, made as I am by Love to respond to love gladly and freely. And so what I do most of the time is a kind of crucifying of myself, my true self, the self I am capable of becoming.

This is simply another way of saying that God's image in me is defaced; but I have been redeemed. And what redemption means is the recovery of something that is meant to be ours.

Dame Julian of Norwich writes:

> The Lord wants us to see our wretchedness and meekly to acknowledge it, but he does not want us to remain there, or to be much occupied in self-accusation, nor does he want us to be too full of our misery. He wants us quickly to attend him. . . and he hastens to bring us to him, for we are his joy and delight, and he is the remedy of our life.

When I look at Jesus I see myself as I might be: what God means by a human being. 'Behold, the Man!' 'The glory of God', said Irenaeus in the second century, 'is a man full-grown.' Jesus is the whole person, the human being who is not damaged or divided or fearful. And when therefore I look at Jesus on the cross, I see what happened once in history to this man who represents me as God intends me to be. I see being acted out once on Calvary what I do to myself day by day. Every day, in all kinds of hidden and open ways, my ego is killing, crucifying, stifling my true self. What I do privately, in all my petty resentments and jealousies and unthoughtful words and unloving actions, this dreadful crucifying of the life of God within me, has been done once openly to Jesus. I look at the cross and know beyond any shadow of doubt what you can do to me, and I to you, and what we each do to ourselves; and we can stop pretending.

So each of us is in a real sense both the one who is crucified and the one who does the crucifying.

But what happens when we contemplate the cross? We hear the words, 'Father, forgive them, for they know not what they do.' No, we don't know what we do to ourselves or each other or the God in whose likeness we are made: this is the deceiving power of sin. But if we look at that naked, bleeding figure, we do know, and we feel sorrow, remorse, guilt. Only to find that our guilt and remorse are met with forgiveness: forgiveness, the readiness to trust someone all over again.

The work of Christ is forgiveness. The cross is the still point of the turning world by which all else is illuminated. This is how God resolves the conflict between his judgement and his compassion: he breaks into history, makes himself known, cuts through all our words with a life that compels silence and response. Here is a mystery of great power, and our job is not so much to explain it as to proclaim it, to proclaim it in our words and in our lives. At its centre, at the point where the cross stands, there are words of love: 'Father, forgive them.' 'It was God', writes St Paul to the Corinthians, 'who reconciled us to himself through Christ, and gave us the work of handing on this reconciliation.'

If I were to sum up in a sentence why I am a Christian, I should have to say that it is because I believe in the Passion of Jesus Christ and the compassion of God – Passion from the Latin *passio*, meaning to suffer, and compassion from *cum passio*, meaning to suffer with or to suffer alongside. That is to say, I see a world that has pain and suffering at its very heart, I believe in a God who loves me beyond my imagining and in a gospel that brings the two together at a place called Calvary.

There is a feeble gospel and there is a powerful gospel. The feeble gospel sees Jesus as our pattern, our example. Such a gospel may not do much harm, but it has no power to change our lives. It leaves you untouched at the centre. But the powerful gospel has at its heart the cross and Passion of Jesus, the compassion of God. It speaks of forgiveness, of death and of new life. The feeble gospel says, 'You may be forgiven.' The powerful gospel says, 'You are redeemed!' And properly to understand the powerful gospel, that of the cross and the resurrection, is to be seized by the vision of a world turned topsy-turvy, a world in which greatness means the service of others and love means the giving of yourself, a world in which the good will be crucified and glory lies in suffering, a world in which finding your life means losing it, a world in which, when judgement and compassion conflict, compassion always wins and forgiveness always, in all ways, has the final word.

Will you receive forgiveness? In Paul Tillich's phrase: 'Will you accept that you are accepted?' For what the cross says is that God, without waiting for repentance, has wrought an act of reconciliation that creates a new relationship between us. The feeble gospel can only preach, 'God is ready to forgive you'; the powerful gospel preaches, 'God has redeemed you' – and that is the good news to which we are called to give attention.

Austin Farrer wrote in one of his finest sermons:

God forgives me with the compassion of his eyes,

when my back is turned to him. I have been told that he forgives me, but I will not turn and have the forgiveness, not though I feel the eyes on my back. God forgives me, for he takes my head between his hands and turns my face to him. And though I struggle against those hands, for they are human, though divine, scarred with nails – though I hurt them, they do not let go until he has smiled me into smiling; and that is the forgiveness of God.

What a way to run a universe! For a God who is Christlike, and whose nature is love, there is no other way possible.

3

Seeing with the Heart

In a previous chapter, I spoke about giving attention to the God who is to be found both in the stillness of our hearts and in the pain and anguish of his creation. Now, I want to ask what it means to give attention to ourselves and to other people: first, to other people, that 'love of neighbour' which is implicit in our faith. Loving, caring, cherishing, affirming, valuing – all words that mean, once again, the giving of attention, in this case, the giving of attention to others.

You and I are surrounded by many people who are angry and confused, often feeling isolated and unloved because they simply don't know who or what they truly are. And they can only find their identity when someone else cares enough to give them attention, when someone else sees them with love. In Arthur Miller's play, *Death of a Salesman*, the central figure is Willie Loman, an unattractive, unsuccessful travelling salesman. At the age of 60, after long years of work and struggle, paying the mortgage, improving his home, he has few real friends, he has grown apart from his two sons and he is despairing at the apparent purposelessness of his life. And his wife, who knows he has been unfaithful to her but who sees him with clear and loving eyes, says this:

> He's not the finest character that ever lived. But he's a human being, and a terrible thing is happening to him. So attention must be paid. He is not to be allowed to fall into his grave like an old dog. Attention, attention must finally be paid to such a person.

In his book *Festival*, Brother Roger, the Founder and Prior of the Taizé Community, writes:

> There are only beautiful faces, be they sad or radiant. My life is discerning in others what is ravishing them, what rejoices them; it lies in communicating with the suffering and the joy of people. Ever since I was a youth, my desire has been never to condemn. For me the essential, in the presence of some other person, has always been to understand him fully. When I manage to

understand somebody, that is already a festival.

That kind of compassionate regard was beautifully described 1600 years ago by one of the Desert Fathers who was really defining compassion when he wrote these words:

> It is right for a person to take up the burden for those who are near to him, whatsoever it may be and, so to speak, to put his own soul in the place of that of his neighbour, and to become, if it were possible, a double man; and he must suffer, and weep, and mourn for him as if he himself had put on the actual body of his neighbour.

I wonder if the monk Thomas Merton knew those words. He had a sudden overwhelming disclosure on a street corner in Louisville, Kentucky:

> In Louisville, at the corner of Fourth and Walnut, in the center of the shopping district, I was suddenly overwhelmed with the realization that I loved all these people, that they were mine and I theirs, that we could not be alien to one another, even though we were total strangers. It was like waking from a dream of separateness . . . to take your place as a member of the human race . . . I

have the immense joy of being *man*, a member of the race in which God himself became incarnate. If only everybody could realize this. But it cannot be explained. There is no way of telling people that they are all walking around shining like the sun.

They say that Van Gogh painted as he did because he wanted to imbue humankind with intimations of immortality. He wrote from Arles,

> I want to paint men and women with that something of the eternal which the halo used to symbolize, and which I seek to convey by the actual radiance and vibration of my colouring.

This attentiveness, this quality of giving attention, is a way of relating not just to the world, but to its people, with love. It involves a kind of dual vision: the ability to see, at one and the same time and with compassion, our human potential and our human sinfulness, the glory to which we are called and the distance we have fallen from that glory.

There is an American writer and artist, Frederick Franck, who writes of this very special way of seeing, which an artist has and which, when it is a question of seeing people, must go hand in hand with compassion. He writes:

> Once you start drawing a face you realize how extraordinary it is – a sheer miracle. While in Rome drawing members of the Vatican Council, I often drew Cardinal Ottaviani. He fascinated me. I saw him as a Grand Inquisitor. He was old and half-blind. One eye was glassy, the other drooped. He had a confusing multiplicity of chins. As I continued drawing him I began to see him differently. Where I had only seen arrogant rigidity and decrepitude, I saw the human being – until I realized that I was seeing him with a kind of love.

Visit any art gallery and see how Rembrandt, or Franz Hals, or Holbein or Cézanne captures the miracle of *this* man or *that* woman because they have given a loving attentiveness to the person who lies before them.

Jesus of Nazareth takes men and women just as they are, human, complex, vulnerable. He at once gives them his whole attention. He starts talking to them and, as he talks, so new perspectives and possibilities open up, for he clearly loves them. He calls them to open their eyes to their true potential and to the love of God; he calls them to renewed attention. And each is enabled to do so because each is himself or herself the focal point of Christ's own loving attention.

All through the Gospels, Jesus invites people to attend to the God who is as much immanent (in the world) as he is transcendent (over and above it), and he draws their attention to the reality deeply hidden in all things and revealed in bread, in water, in a flower, in a face. He draws their attention to the mystery, to the beyond, that which is deeper, higher, more intimate, yet he keeps them firmly rooted in their daily lives. And in being attentive to what Jesus says and does, they find they are then being attentive to God.

Jesus didn't speak much about people seeing God, but over and over again he pictured God at the heart of their ordinary experience, in scenes like that of children playing in the market place, or guests at a wedding or farmers sowing in their fields. There the ordinary becomes the way into the extraordinary.

There's a story which Charles Raven, who was both a scientist and a priest, used to tell. He was walking back from Liverpool Cathedral on a winter evening in the early thirties when there was a severe depression in Lancashire and many people were hungry, and he passed a crowded fish-and-chip shop. The sight of the shop, with the ritual of scooping out the chips and emptying them onto the greaseproof paper, was familiar enough, but suddenly it took on a new significance, and of it he wrote: 'All of a sudden, I saw the *glory* . . . The ordinary became the extraordinary; in that context the proprietor symbolized the heavenly Father giving his children their daily bread.'

The French Roman Catholic priest, Yves Raquin writes: 'Embedded in every event and in every human being, lies hidden a pearl that glows only for those who pay attention.' So we are back to giving attention to whatever and whoever is before us in this present moment, really looking at a person so that we may feel something of the force and great mystery of their existence, however damaged and spoiled they may be. Jesus looks at the flower or the sparrow, and they speak to him of the love and care of the Father. He looks at the world, and it speaks to him of the kingdom of God. He looks at individuals and knows them for what they are but sees them for what they shall be, and he comes to open our eyes that we may see as he sees. He comes to give sight to the blind.

And it is the task of the Holy Spirit not only to open our eyes that we may see the world as God's world, but to open our eyes so that we may see one another as the uniquely valued children of God. There is a small incident in St Mark's Gospel in which Jesus heals a man born blind that neatly bridges the gap between the world of nature and the world of persons, for it's about seeing people as trees or seeing them as people. The story is a kind of parable. Jesus takes the blind man by the hand, puts spittle on his eyes, lays his hands on him and then asks, 'Can you see anything?' 'I can see people, but they look like trees and they are walking about.' Trees – not necessarily just green things that stand in the way, for trees are beautiful and can move you to tears of joy – nevertheless they are things, objects without feelings. Then Jesus lays his hands on his eyes again, and he can see clearly. And Jesus says to the disciples, 'Do you not yet understand? Have you no perception? Are your minds closed? Have you eyes that do not see and ears that do not hear?'

Interestingly, that story of the healing of the blind man is told by St Mark between the feeding of the five thousand with the consequent failure of the disciples to understand what this sign is saying about Jesus as the living bread (they were only concerned about the shortage of food) and the incident at Caesarea Philippi where Jesus asks his disciples who he is, and only Peter has the perception to say 'You are the Messiah'. And what both these stories declare is that there is a seeing with the eyes and a seeing with the heart and the understanding.

A seeing with the heart. A being born from above. A seeing in the light of the Holy Spirit, a looking at the world and seeing it full of God's glory: a looking at Jesus and seeing in him what human beings mean by God and what God means by a human being, and a looking at your neighbour and seeing not a walking tree, but an individual made like you in the image of God, unique and therefore irreplaceable. It was Gandhi who wrote: 'If you don't find God in the very next person you meet, it is a waste of time looking for him further.'

But there is one further thing to say. For supremely and primarily the Holy Spirit opens our eyes to Christ. Not just to Jesus of Nazareth, who was once met and listened to and followed at a certain point in history, but to the living Christ, here and now. The

Christ in each other. We can no longer experience Jesus as a man as the disciples did, but we can encounter Christ as a life-giving Spirit. Once the ascension has taken place, once he has returned to the Father, once there is no person to see and hear, then his followers have to look for him elsewhere. They have to turn and look into one another's eyes, listen to one another's words, receive forgiveness from one another's lips and receive the broken bread at one another's hands. It is here now that the Christ is chiefly to be recognized and found. Within his body, the church, but not by any means exclusively here. We have to find him incarnate in our neighbour, and not least in the suffering bodies of the poor, the hungry, the outcast and the imprisoned.

I once heard Archbishop Derek Worlock describing a visit he made to a shanty town in Peru. In a clay lean-to that served as a chapel, he spotted a small boy sitting in the semi-darkness. The priest asked his name. 'Jesus,' he replied. The priest smiled and asked him if he knew who the first Jesus was. The boy thought, pointed his finger at himself and said 'Me'. Then he got up and shambled out, dragging a paralysed arm and leg. 'We found out later', said Archbishop Worlock, 'that this was the result of a dirty syringe used by a relief agency inoculating the area.'

Now this mystery of the indwelling Christ, or the *imago Dei*, the image of the Christlike God in human beings, is a mystery that is hard to explain in imprecise, slippery words, but the New Testament is full of it. It is the mystery of Jesus' own promise, 'I am with you always'; the mystery spoken of in the fourth Gospel of the vine and the branches, 'I am in you and you in me'. It is the mystery of St Paul's claim, 'I live, yet not I, but Christ lives in me', of his words to the Corinthians that 'you ought to know by this time that Christ is in you, unless you are not a real Christian at all.'

Jesus said, 'You have eyes: can you not see?' Every Christian is called to a ministry of compassion – and especially to those wounded and often pretty unattractive individuals who can be greatly supported and upheld if one person is prepared to give them attention and see them not just as they are but as they might be. Sometimes we may feel our attempt to love individuals like this to be so small and trivial and unimportant compared with the huge issues, the massive disasters, of our world. But always remember this: Jesus devoted himself to the small successes and the small failures of individual men and women. No doubt the Pharisees and the Zealots and the Essenes spent hour upon hour debating those movements and courses which affected the life of the nation. Jesus, on the other hand, gives his attention to the woman of Samaria, to the blind beggar, to Martha and Mary, to Zacchaeus and the woman taken in adultery – for the key to the Christian understanding of the many is the value and unique worth of each one.

This is the most important and miraculous opening of our eyes by the Spirit: when the figure of Jesus in history and in the church is encountered in and through each other as the living, life-giving Christ. And I want to leave you with an image, something I saw in Calcutta some years ago, which I have never been able to forget. I was in Calcutta making a radio programme about the work of Mother Teresa, who says when she feeds the starving destitute and cares for the dying that she is serving Jesus 'under the distressing disguise of the poor'. That's an interesting phrase. I was in the Home for Dying Destitutes, being taken round by the sister in charge, Sister Luke. The hospice is very simple: two wards, one for men, one for women and children. Sister Luke took me across to a small alcove, which lay between them. She drew back a plastic curtain. In a stone trough, two of the sisters were gently washing the naked, dirty, stick-like body of a woman who had just been brought in from the street. Over their heads, written in simple letters of a card and stuck to the wall, were the four words: 'The Body of Christ.'

4

A True and Proper Self-Regard

Here is a prayer of Harry Williams:

> Hello, it is me,
> your old friend and your old enemy,
> your loving friend who often neglects you,
> your complicated friend,
> your utterly perplexed and decidedly resentful
>   friend,
> partly loving, partly hating, partly not caring.
> It is me.

Earlier I was talking about love in terms of giving attention to our neighbour, about valuing and affirming each other. But I cannot even begin to love my neighbour unless I have first learned to love myself. I am to love my neighbour as I love myself. And so I want to think with you about what it means to give proper attention to your self. For not only are we, in William Blake's phrase, to learn to see with 'our doors of perception cleansed', but we have also, in Ezekiel's words, to be 'full of eyes within'.

I spoke a bit earlier of the many people who feel unvalued and unloved, who have never been on the receiving end of being loved for their own sake – not even as a child. Somehow, they need to discover, perhaps with our help, how to become what each one truly is, a uniquely valuable and valued child of God.

But I have to discover it first as it applies to me. I have to learn and relearn and learn again this truth as it speaks to me until it is as natural to me as breathing if I am to be of any use to others as a healer and a reconciler. It isn't that I am not wounded, vulnerable and human – it's that I have accepted in the very deepest part of my being that I am accepted, redeemed and loved, not in spite of being me but *because* I am me.

I have to discover that my Father loves me every bit as much when I am sinful as when I am loving, that he delights in me because I am me. To claim that God in Jesus Christ loves us for ourselves and has forgiven and accepted us *as we are* is of course an overwhelming, and to many a rather shocking, reversal of all reasonable religious protocol. Well, so it is. Thank God, so it is. But it's the gospel.

So what of this 'self' that God appears to love and I am commanded to love as well, this self, of which I am conscious of about two per cent, the rest lying buried deep in my subconscious, though like an iceberg capable of inflicting powerful damage?

In his brief and jewel-like essay 'On the Love of God', St Bernard of Clairvaux distinguishes four degrees of love: The first degree is the love of self *for self*. 'We have indeed', he writes, 'no feeling that is not for self. For whoever hated his own flesh?' The second degree is the love of God *for what he gives us*: 'Man begins by loving God, not for God's sake but for his own', he writes. The third degree of love is love of God *for what he is*. And the fourth degree is love both of self and of neighbour wholly *for God's sake*.

St Bernard does not see this fourth degree of love as being reached this side of heaven. And yet, even when we have become thoroughly at one with God, this highest degree of love is still *love of self* for God's sake.

The monk, Thomas Merton, has this to say about those words of St Bernard:

These words show that the fulfilment of our destiny is not merely to be lost in God, as the traditional figures of speech would have it, like a 'drop of water in a barrel of wine or like iron in the fire' but found in God in all our individual and personal reality, tasting our eternal happiness not only in the fact that we have attained to the possession of his infinite goodness, but above all in the fact that we see his will done in us.

Let me repeat that truth. We shall find our eternal happiness in the fact that we have finally allowed God's will to be done in us 'in all our individual and personal reality'. Understand *that* and we shall realize why it matters so much that I value – indeed, that I love – myself. And the key to our understanding lies not just in seeing that we human beings are embodied spirits, capable, like God, of self-giving love, not just in realizing that we are capable of creating (as artists do) beauty and order out of chaos. It is the realization that each one of us is literally irreplaceable. I have my own special identity that can never to replicated, not in a million years. What makes me unique and irreplaceable is not that I have special gifts and characteristics to offer that glitter like the silver balls on a Christmas tree. Rather it lies in my own personal, intimate relationship with

God, which is mine and mine alone, and it is this that makes me precious in his sight.

I am me. You are you. A real, distinctive individual, 'warts and all', and what makes me sometimes difficult to take and what makes me sometimes lovable is my own individuality. The call to 'become what I am', to grow in the image and likeness of God as we see that in Christ, doesn't mean losing my self, in a frightening kind of self-abasing abandonment. It means discovering at last what it means to be *me*, open at last to God's illuminating and transforming and affirming Spirit. Just as, within the relationship of marriage or a deep friendship, the more you give yourself away in the give and take of love, the more your individual identity and worth is enhanced. Those who wish to gain their lives must be prepared to give them away.

Here is a truth that applies to every living thing – to a tree, a hazelnut, a tiger, a person – a truth that recognizes the fact that no two snowflakes are alike. Everything is uniquely itself, there in its own right, to do its own thing, to be recognized and celebrated in the moment that is now by those with eyes to see. There is a passage in the book of Revelation that reads: 'To him who proves victorious I will give a white stone with a new name on it, known only to the person who receives it.' To be given that white stone with a new name upon it is, I suppose, to find your soul, finally to discover your true unique identity. And if we believe that God is not the God of the dead but of the living, then we believe that when I speak of my soul I speak of myself as irreplaceable, and that God will maintain or re-create this irreplaceable person who is me in and through the death of my body. For each of us is no less important in God's eyes than we are in our own, and one day we shall see ourselves (and our neighbour) as God sees us and love ourselves (and our neighbour) for God's sake.

I find this concept of irreplaceability a very helpful one. Please God, we already know what it may mean in terms of ourselves and those we love. We are called to make an act of faith that everybody is irreplaceable, every human being a person in this special sense. Helen Oppenheimer writes in one of her books:

Everyone can agree that Michelangelo is irreplaceable, but when God says of a drunken tramp, 'but I loved that one. I did not want him lost', God's other children must try to see this point. We should see it, after all, if the tramp's mother said it. What belief in a heavenly Father requires is the exercise of imagination to see each other's irreplaceability as well as our own.

Now if I seem to be asserting the importance of self-love, *my* uniqueness in God's sight, even though it includes your unique value too, it may not seem to sit easily beside Christ's insistence on self-denial. Surely *agape*, selfless love, is at the very heart of our faith? Yes, of course, but I am not arguing for selfishness, simply for the proper valuing of myself. We are not in the business of self-hatred or a destructive self-negation. In seeking to put God first, what we are seeking is not negation but fulfilment – me becoming what I truly am. And I shall learn to become what I truly am by giving proper attention to God and by giving attention to my neighbour, by cherishing and affirming them; and you, my neighbour, will become what you truly are by cherishing and affirming me. And the affirming of our value, in the light of Good Friday and Easter – the affirming of my significance as well as yours – is as much part of the authentic Christian tradition as the theme of self-denial. There is a true and proper self-regard, a delight in what the incarnate God has done in me. A delight that I am redeemed, forgiven and set free. A delight that my body is a temple of the Holy Spirit.

It is to insult God to view ourselves with less compassion than that with which he views us, or indeed with which we view our neighbour. For the simple fact is that we cannot love others unless we first know the meaning of loving ourselves. If we are to see others as lovable, we can't opt out of being lovable too. Once you believe that someone is fond of you, you will be more encouraged to become what they want and need you to be. For that is the divine order: 'We love', says St John, 'because he first loved us.' So I repeat, what makes each one of us of irreplaceable value is that I am of irreplaceable value to God, not because I am attractive or loving or gifted or even worthy of his love. I may be none of these things and certainly can never be the latter. But that is how God is. He sees me as I could be, but he accepts me as I am.

There is, then, a proper self-love – a giving attention to yourself that is not self-indulgence. It is rather an honest assessment of who you are, an honest recognition of your sinfulness and God's grace, a proper understanding of your own irreplaceable value – and mine – and his – and hers – in God's sight. This proper giving attention to yourself is to accept that people will have expectations of you, but also to be able to judge which expectations are valid.

It is to accept the hurt you carry, the pain you have known. And it is to recognize that, if you face this pain, you can make your very weakness a source of strength, for you may then be able to speak out of your own hurt or loneliness to others who face a bleak suffering they cannot understand. Not to parade such feelings; not to say, 'I know exactly how you feel'. I am speaking of something infinitely subtler than that: of how it is possible to speak with the authenticity of a human being who knows their own vulnerability and bears their own scars.

So then, whoever you are, whatever your strengths and weaknesses, no one else can be to certain other people what you are to them. You can't be cloned; no one can replace you. Your relationship with those you love is yours and yours alone. Nurture those relationships, and from the bottom of your heart thank God that, although you are (in Harry Williams's words) 'neglectful, complicated, often perplexed and sometimes resentful, partly loving, partly hating, partly not caring', nevertheless, by God's grace, you are able to say: I am baptized. I am loved. I am a member of the constantly forgiven, ever-renewed eucharistic community. And I am, at this very instant and at every instant of my life, in a relationship with God in Christ that transcends time and space and is therefore eternal. And God calls me, gently, persistently, every day of my life, to give attention to what I am so that I may give attention to what others are too, and so, little by little, become what I truly am until the day when 'I wake up after his likeness and am satisfied at it'.

Index of Biblical References

Index of Names